THE GNOSTIC ATTITUDE

by

Geo Widengren

translated from the Swedish

and edited by

Birger A. Pearson

WIPF & STOCK · Eugene, Oregon

Wipf and Stock Publishers
199 W 8th Ave, Suite 3
Eugene, OR 97401

The Gnostic Attitude by Geo Widengren
Translated from the Swedish and Edited by Birger Pearson
By Widengren, Geo and Pearson, Birger A.
Copyright©1973 by Pearson, Birger A.
ISBN 13: 978-1-62564-732-0
Publication date 2/26/2014
Previously published by Institute of Religious Studies, 1973

TRANSLATOR'S PREFACE

During the Spring quarter of 1972, Professor Geo
Widengren of Uppsala University in Sweden, one of the
truly great historians of religion of our time, was in
Santa Barbara as Visiting Professor in the Department
of Religious Studies of the University of California,
and Research Scholar in the Institute of Religious
Studies of the University. Toward the end of his
sojourn here I indicated to him that I would like to
see the chapter on Gnosticism in his widely-acclaimed
book, *Religionens värld*, translated into English and
published as a separate essay. Having devoted a number of years to the scholarly study of ancient
Gnosticism, I had long been interested in what Widengren
has written on this subject. So I expressed to him my
willingness, even eagerness, to translate this chapter
in his phenomenological opus myself, and to see it
through the press. He was quite willing to have this
done, and the present work is the result.

This translation from Widengren's elegant Swedish
was done in rough draft beneath the towering, luxuriant
redwoods of coastal California, while on vacation in
the Santa Cruz Mountains. From such a vantage point
one is more inclined to praise the Creator of this

world than to deprecate him, to rejoice in the beauty
of his handiwork than to regard it anxiously as a
baneful prison.

Nevertheless there is a widespread current of
feeling in the Western world (not only in Southern
California!) that is quite comparable to that "spirit
of late antiquity" ("Spätantiker Geist", a phrase used
by Hans Jonas) from which the various gnostic sects
of the early centuries of our era were nourished: a
feeling of world-weariness, of powerlessness in the
face of dark and impersonal forces at loose in the
social and political arena, a fascination with the
occult and with esoteric lore, a quest for meaning in
the face of meaninglessness, and a search for ego
identity. I have found in my own teaching in the
university that students are very interested in
Gnosticism in all of its various aspects. Some
students, I am pleased to say, are even willing to
study the ancient languages, e.g. Greek, Latin, even
Coptic, in order to be able to read the original texts
and sources.

It is therefore in the interests of college and
university students primarily that I have prepared this
translation. Among scholars, Geo Widengren is the
foremost proponent of the thesis that Gnosticism is
rooted in the religious speculations of ancient India
and Iran. What he has written in this essay is a

summary of a great deal of scholarly work scattered in many publications, a succinct statement of his interpretation of the gnostic phenomenon. As such it commends itself to students interested in the various approaches to the study of Gnosticism, and of religion in general. I am eager to have my own students read Widengren's essay, not least because his approach differs somewhat from my own; for it will provide for them a wider context from which to approach the subject.

This translation is based on the latest Swedish edition of *Religionens värld* (Stockholm, 1971). It must be pointed out, however, that this edition is completely without footnotes. The footnotes for the present work have been prepared by me, largely on the basis of Widengren's footnotes in the German translation of his book, *Religionsphänomenologie* (Berlin, 1969). The German translation of this chapter on Gnosticism does not contain the section dealing with the poet Eric Johan Stagnelius, but it does include at certain points material that has been abbreviated out of the Swedish edition. In most cases this extra material from the German has been included here, either in the text itself or in footnotes. In addition, I have edited the translation in such a way that cross-references in the text itself to other chapters of the book have been omitted so as to allow this chapter to stand on its own as a separate essay. Such references, with page notations to both the German and the Swedish editions of the book, are preserved here in the footnotes.

In some cases, duly noted in footnotes, I have used standard English translations in quotations from ancient primary sources. Otherwise the English translation of such sources has been made directly from the Swedish or, in the case of material in the footnotes, from the German. An attempt has been made to check such quotations against the respective ancient versions themselves. Thus Greek, Latin, Coptic, and Arabic sources have been so checked (the Arabic materials by my colleague, Charles Wendell). The whole thing has subsequently been read by Professor Widengren, and minor changes and additions to the notes suggested by him have been incorporated.

One further comment on the translation: My poor attempt to render into English the haunting beauty of Eric Johan Stagnelius' verses is by no means -- alas! -- a claim to have shared in the great poet's Muse!

It is a pleasure to register here my appreciation to those who have assisted in my labors. One of my students, Miss Judy Saltzmann, had prepared a working translation of the German version of this chapter for a course she took from Widengren in the spring of 1972. I found it useful to compare my work with hers. My colleague, Torborg Lundell, checked my

translations of Stagnelius and offered some helpful
suggestions; I am grateful to her for this. Another
colleague, Gerald Larson, offered some useful suggestions
pertaining to the Indian materials, for which I thank
him. Yet another colleague, Charles Wendell, not only
checked the Arabic materials for me, but also supplied
some important references for me on the basis of a
visit to the UCLA library. My hearty thanks go to
him, also. My colleague, Walter Capps, Director of
the Institute of Religious Studies, has been unstinting
in his support of this project. For accepting this
work as the first number in this series of Institute
papers -- and for a close personal friendship of long
standing -- I am grateful to him. To Miss Kay Elmore
of the Department of Religious Studies staff, for her
typing of the penultimate manuscript, I tender my
sincere thanks. The present form of the monograph
reflects the typing skill of Mrs. Martha Saunders
Oppenheim, secretary to the Institute of Religious
Studies and a graduate student in the Department; I am
grateful to her for her fine work. Mr. Ernst F. Tonsing,
Research Associate of the Institute and a graduate
student of mine in the Department, suggested the cover
design, and has assisted in numerous ways in the pro-
duction of this work. I tender him my sincere thanks.

Finally, to Professor Geo Widengren, I express my
heartfelt appreciation, not only for the depth and the

breadth of his scholarship -- an inspiration to us
all -- but also for the warm personal friendship that
has grown up between us. *Må han leva uti hundrade år!*

Santa Barbara

November, 1972

ACKNOWLEDGMENTS

Acknowledgment is due the following for kind per-
mission to quote: Holt, Rinehart & Winston for the
quotation from Eliot Deutsch's translation of the
Bhagavad Gita which appears on p. 40 f.; Macmillan for
the quotation from Arberry's translation of the Koran
on p. 68, n. 76; and Oxford University Press for the
quotations from Hume's translation of the Upanishads
on pp. 3, 4, 5, and 15.

ABBREVIATIONS

ARW	*Archiv für Religionswissenschaft*
BSO(A)S	*Bulletin of the School of Oriental (and African) Studies*
CG	*Cairensis Gnosticus*
ERE	Hastings' *Encyclopaedia of Religion and Ethics*
JA	*Journal Asiatique*
JRASB	*Journal of the Royal Asiatic Society, Bombay Branch*
Le Origini	U. Bianchi, ed., *Le Origini dello gnosticismo*
MO	*Le Monde Oriental. Revue des études orientales*
NTS	*New Testament Studies*
OLZ	*Orientalische Literaturzeitung*
RSV	Revised Standard Version of the Bible
SBE	Sacred Books of the East
WZKM	*Wiener Zeitschrift für die Kunde des Morgenlandes*
ZDMG	*Zeitschrift der deutschen morganländischen Gesellschaft*
ZII	*Zeitschrift für Indologie und Iranistik*
ZNW	*Zeitschrift für die neutestamentliche Wissenschaft und die Kunde der älteren Kirche*

ZPE   *Zeitschrift für Papyrologie und Epigraphik*
ZRGG   *Zeitschrift für Religions- und Geistes-*
          geschichte

THE GNOSTIC ATTITUDE*

The Indo-Iranian Background

1. The cosmological basis of gnostic religion is rooted
in Indo-Iranian pantheistic speculation, wherein God
and the world are regarded as one.[1] The higher life-
principle in man, Indian *ātman*, Iranian *manah*, is
identical to the spiritual principle in the Universe,
in India the Great Ātman or Brahman, in Iran the Great
Vohu Manah. The higher element in man is thus a part
of the Deity's spiritual Ego, while man's body consti-
tutes a part of the divine body, the world. This kind
of monistic pantheistic speculation could, however,
develop in a dualistic direction.[2] When it is disputed
that there is multiplicity in the universe, and it is
insisted that there is only a unity (Puruṣa, the Great
Ātman), one is led in India to conceive of the actually
existing multiplicity as mere appearance.[3] At first
this was by no means the case. Multiplicity was regarded as identical to the One and therefore as real.
But in multiplicity, according to this view, there was
nothing that was not the One. Herein lay the starting
point for further speculation along these lines. For
if multiplicity in reality was the One, the undeniable

1

consequence must be that multiplicity only *appears* as multiplicity, that it is, so to speak, an illusion.

Already several hundred years before Shankara, whose religious philosophy applied in a thoroughgoing way the doctrine of multiplicity as a product of illusion, *māyā*, there had been coined a famous simile subsequently repeated often: As in the dark one might take a rope for a snake, so it is with the divine One. In its place there is manifest unbounded multiplicity:

> This is God's Māyā, through which he
> deceives himself.

It is *māyā*, illusion, which produces the empty appearance of the phenomenal world.

During the Upanishadic period, according to Oldenberg, there existed only the starting points for such a conception but not this conception itself.[4] Of essential significance, however, is the attitude toward the multiplicity of phenomena. How does one stand with respect to the phenomenal world? Oldenberg rightly points out that the basic insight which traces multiplicity back to the unity of Brahman-Ātman had a decisive effect upon the evaluation of existence. Two possibilities presented themselves here -- which is always the case with a pantheistic speculation: *Either* one emphasized the proposition that the world is identical with Brahman and is permeated by him. In that

2

case the world must take part in the value which is
ascribed to Brahman. *Or* one attached decisive significance to the proposition that multiplicity, as a
derivation of the One, constituted a divergence from
the One, a defection, and therefore represented some-
how an antithesis to the One. In the latter case a
negative evaluation of existence was the result.[5]
Oldenberg points out that there was no lack of attempts
at a solution to the problem in a positive direction.
Nevertheless an optimistic evaluation of existence is
surely overshadowed by the pessimistic interpretation
of the world of exterior phenomena.[6]

Oldenberg was of the opinion that the prospect of
death had the greatest influence upon the development
of speculation in the direction of a pessimistic evaluation of the world. Death appeared as the absolute
evil. An expression was coined quite early and often
repeated, "Death, the evil". One would say, "May not
the evil, death, reach me!" And one would pray,

> From the unreal (*asat*) lead me to
> the real (*sat*)!
> From darkness lead me to light!
> From death lead me to immortality!
> --*Bṛhad-Āraṇyaka Upaniṣad* 1.3.28[7]

The explanation of this Vedic saying which follows
in this passage is that the unreal and darkness are

3

death, while the real and the light are immortality. In contrast to Ātman with its predicate light, glory, immortality, and blessedness, stands this world as the quintessence of darkness and death. "Everything here is overtaken by death, since everything is overcome by death" (*Bṛhad-Āranyaka Upaniṣad* 3.1.3). Therefore bodily existence itself is given over to death.[8]

> This body is mortal. It has been
> appropriated by Death. [But] it is
> the standing-ground of that death-
> less, bodiless Self (*Ātman*). Verily,
> he who is incorporate has been appro-
> priated by pleasure and pain. Verily,
> there is no freedom from pleasure and
> pain for one while he is incorporate.
> Verily, while one is bodiless, pleasure
> and pain do not touch him.
>   --*Chāndogya Upaniṣad* 8.12.1

What a contrast between the universal Ātman sur-rounded by life, light, and glory on the one hand, and the world given over to death and darkness on the other! And we see, too, how the macrocosm-microcosm specula-tion applies here. For the same antithesis pertains also in the contrast between the immortal, incorporeal Ātman in man, and his body which is given over to desire, pain, and death. Of *ātman* it is said,

4

He is your soul, which is in all things.
Aught else than Him [or, than this] is
wretched.

　　--Bṛhad-Āraṇyaka Upaniṣad 3.4.2

From this body of suffering and death in a world
of suffering and death one is to go to the All-One, to
Ātman, in which consciousness is obliterated, so that
there is no longer duplicity, no antithesis to the
all-embracing Ātman (Bṛhad-Āraṇyaka Upaniṣad 2.4.12-
14). The individual ātman-s thus return to the place
whence they had come, to the Great Ātman-Brahman.

2. From this starting point there is developed in
India a more or less dualistically-oriented world view,
for which the way is prepared by Shankara, which is
carried further by Rāmānuja, and which is full-blown
in the direction that bhakti (devotion) takes after
him. The world is apprehended as something split-off
from the divine, created by the deity as the place of
residence for the individual souls which go out from
the divine and return again to him. Rāmānuja's system,
to be sure, intends to be monistic, to the extent that
everything exterior returns to Brahman. But the
existence of the exterior world and of the individual
soul is not denied, and the relation of matter to
Brahman presents certain difficulties for Rāmānuja.[9]

An interesting moment portrayed in the Upanishads with typical Indian rhetoric is the occasion when the soul, at the time of its heavenly journey up to Brahman's dwelling-place, comes to *Brahmaloka*, the Brahma-world. Upon entry the soul is met by female divine beings, *Apsaras*, with fruits, unguents, wreaths, garments, and sweet-smelling powder. They adorn him as Brahma him- self. The soul is thus given the same garment as the deity himself, the world-mantle.[10]

We observe here a relationship which we shall run across again and again. Brahma has the world as his body, as has already been pointed out. Here, however, the world appears as his garment. We thus see how "body" and "garment" are two completely synonymous expressions in the language of symbol. The soul enters the palace with its vestibule and approaches the dwelling-place and throne of Brahma.[11] Here we have the doctrine of the soul's heavenly journey, so full of significance for further developments in Iranian religion and in gnostic religion generally.[12]

The way up to Brahman is not without danger, nor without toil can one reach the *brahmaloka*. One must have gods as guardians along the way, and heavenly troops as escorts. One must be furnished with fare for the journey -- that is a conception which later recurs often in the Buddhist texts. When one enters the higher world, one is united with the treasure of

6

his alms and good works -- that is an idea that is
expressed already in the *Rigveda* 10.14.8. This conception of the treasure of good works one finds also
in the Buddhist texts (e.g., *Samyutta-Nikāya* 3.14).
According to *Vājasaneyīsamhitā* 18.64, man's good works
are guarded in heaven by the gods. It is, therefore,
not remarkable that the ancient High-god Prajāpati
himself is called the "Treasurer" (*Taittiriya-brāhmana*
2.8.1.3). In the same scripture (3.10.11.2) it is
stated that man owns in the other world a treasure
which, however, is consumed if the owner lacks knowledge.[13]

According to Indian thought, moreover, salvation
from existence in this world with its darkness and
death comes about as a result of insight, *jnāna*. The
way to salvation, as pointed out in the Upanishads, is
called "the way of insight", *jnānamārga*.[14] We note
also the meaning carried by the term "salvation" here,
mukti or *moksa*.[15] Salvation, *mukti*, means release
from the body and unity with Brahman in absolute one-
ness with him. *Mukti* means that man is freed from the
veil of ignorance, *avidyā*, "not-knowing", which con-
ceals from the soul that it is, indeed, one with
Brahman. Salvation signifies a realization of the
insight that our real nature is identical to Brahman.[16]

We have already alluded to the occurrence in
ancient Iran of the pantheistic speculation, the es-
sentials of which constitute the basis for the salvation

7

doctrine of the Upanishads and the religious philoso-
phies dependent upon them. The question, therefore,
is to what extent one finds again the soteriological
concepts which we have discussed thus far. It seems
appropriate to take as a point of departure the doctrine of the heavenly journey of the soul, a central
dogma of salvation in Iranian religion.

The credit for having discovered the resemblance,
in concrete details, between the description of the
soul's heavenly journey in Iran and in India goes to
S. Wikander. He has pointed to the passage in *Vīdēvdāt*
(19.31-32) where Vohu Manah greets the human soul as
it enters heaven and leads it to Ahura Mazda's golden
throne. In addition to the throne, we encounter also
in the older Iranian texts the garment, Vohu Manah's
garment, which, as Wikander shows, is nothing else than
the world-mantle.[17] In the Zoroastrian Pahlavi scriptures concerning the journeys to heaven and hell
undertaken by the visionary Ardai Viraz, Wikander has
also referred to the passage where the soul receives
a golden throne and Vohu Manah's garment. In later
Manichaean texts in the Middle-Persian language one
finds again, besides the garment and the throne, even
the wreath and the hall through which the soul has to
pass upon his arrival at the divine dwelling.[18] The
relationship in that case between the Manichaean texts
and the ancient Zoroastrian sources, on the one hand,

8

and the texts from the Upanishads, on the other -- a relationship which pertains also to the cosmological speculations[19] -- demonstrates that the gnostic conceptions appearing in Manichaeism have not simply an Iranian, but also an Indo-Iranian, background.[20]

We have seen that the individual man's higher ego, *manah*, the mind, is to be united with the divine *manah*, the cosmic Vohu Manah. This unification is expressed very graphically: the soul is endowed with Vohu Manah's garment, the world-mantle, receives a wreath, and takes its place upon Ahura Mazda's golden throne.

3. Does this heavenly journey of the soul away from the material world, and its entry into the great collective *manah*, have already in ancient Iran the character of salvation from the world as from something evil? We must remember that the conceptions analyzed here are not characteristic of the religion founded by Zarathustra. To the extent that they appear in Zoroastrianism, they are to be regarded as remnants of Iranian folk-religion (understanding by the term "folk-religion" such forms of Iranian religion as stood alongside of the Mazda faith reformed by Zarathustra).[21]

We note, first, of all, that the pessimistic world-view, so dominant in the Upanishads, recurs even

in Iran, *viz.* in the religion of Zervan. This sentiment
is dominated by a cosmological perspective. In the
myth, Zervan is father of the twins Ohrmizd and Ahriman,
of which the latter, the evil power, is lord over the
present world and over the present age.[22] The texts
in *Bundahišn* establish without any doubt that Ahriman's
creation is characterized by darkness and death.
Ahriman himself is surrounded by darkness, *tārīkīh*,
and possessed of a lust for murder, *zatār-kāmakīh*, down
in the depths where he is detained. His garment is
murder-lust, and darkness is his place. Therefore his
place can be referred to as the unbounded darkness,
asar tarīkīh. In contrast, Ohrmizd represents goodness,
vēhīh, and light, *rōšnīh*. This light is Ohrmizd's
throne, *gāh*, and place, *gyāk*. Ohrmizd has charge over
goodness, and omniscience is his garment.[23]

Thus we find here the same contrast as in the
Upanishads, only in much sharper form. Between Ohrmizd
and Ahriman a conflict rages; the powers of light and
darkness wage warfare with each other.[24] Man finds
himself here on earth in a world consisting of mixture,
gumēčišn, of good and evil. But besides this pair of
contrasts, good and evil, there is yet another, heavenly and earthly, *mēnōk-gētīk*. It is worth observing,
however, that in the Zoroastrian texts the dualism of
good-evil does not coincide with the antithesis of
heavenly-earthly, as though the heavenly were the good

10

and the earthly the evil. On the contrary, it is a marked characteristic of Zoroastrianism -- derived from Zarathustra himself -- that the antithesis of good-evil coincides with the antithesis of life-not life, and of light-darkness.[25] Yet if in Zoroastrian religion there is no particular pessimism expressed with respect to bodily existence in and of itself, a mood of pessimistic escape from the world can be found even in Zoroastrianized texts which can be accounted for, e.g., with reference to Zervanite circles. As Nyberg has put it,

"A strong longing for the beyond can occasionally come to expression. The first line in the Avesta tractate *Aogemadaēčā*, which may have been used as a ritual for the dead, is rendered rather freely in the Pahlavi translation in the following way: 'I come, I receive, I am content.' This is paraphrased: 'I come to this world, I receive misfortune, I am content with death.' Longing for the heavenly, transcendental world has doubtless been strongly pronounced among the Iranians throughout their history."[26]

In the Sassanian period this pessimism meets us in Burzoe's introduction to *Kalila wa Dimna*.[27] How much stronger must not this mood be in an Iranian religion such as Zervanism, wherein the representative of evil, Ahriman, is thought to rule over this world! It is especially significant that new Zervanite documents

11

allow us to understand even more clearly how world-denying this religion had been, with its loathing of the female sex and the sexual factor in human existence.[28]

4. We have thus seen that there existed both in India and in Iran the cosmological and psychological premises for the development of a radical dualism, a dualism which equates the world with evil and regards the origin of the material world as a result of the activity of the evil power. Such a view is called "Gnosticism", after the Greek word *gnosis*. Adherents of the gnostic religion called themselves "gnostics", for they considered themselves to possess *gnosis*, knowledge. The characteristic of this knowledge is that it bestows salvation. Insight concerning the nature of the world and of man frees man from the material world, from slavery in the fetters of matter in which his higher life-principle, the divine spirit, is held captive. We have already noted that in Upanishadic speculation the way of knowledge, *jñānamārga*, is the way by which salvation can be attained. So also in Gnosticism the way to salvation is through salvific knowledge. This *gnosis* consists in insight concerning "what we were, what we became; where we were, whither we have been cast; whither we hasten, whence we are delivered; what birth is, what rebirth."[29] This formula is evidently only an expansion of an originally Iranian formulation

12

found, together with other questions, in the Zoroastrian
catechism, *Pandnāmak*:

> Who am I?
>
> To whom do I belong?
>
> Whence have I come?
>
> Whither shall I return?
>
> --*Pandnāmak* ch. 3 [30]

These questions are answered as follows:

> From the heavenly world have I come,
>
> and through matter have I not come into being . . .
>
> I belong to Ohrmizd, not to Ahriman,
>
> to the angels, not to the devils,
>
> to the good, not to evil.
>
> --*Pandnāmak* ch. 5

The question whither the Zoroastrian believer shall
return is answered in the following manner:

> And know that the place of Paradise is
> the best,
>
> and the city of the heavenly world most
> joyful,
>
> and heaven's landscape most luminous,
>
> and the dwelling of luminous Garodman
> most glorious,
>
> and that the pursuit of virtue means
> the greatest hope

for 'the future body' which is
imperishable.

--*Pandnāmak* ch. 31[31]

Man thus comes from the heavenly world, and thither,
to the luminous Garodman, paradise (referred to already
in the Gathas), he has hope to be able to return, if
he pursues the good work of virtue. In the city (or
kingdom) of the heavenly world he receives "the future
body" which is imperishable. While he is in this world,
the Zoroastrian believer belongs to Ohrmizd, not to
Ahriman. We also observe that, even in Zoroastrianism,
great stress is laid upon insight and knowledge concerning man's real destiny. This is especially clear
precisely in this catechism. Salvation, too, plays a
large role, and, characteristically enough, it is the
soul to which salvation applies. It is the soul that
is to be saved from hell and come to paradise.[32] The
term "salvation", *bōžišn*, plays a particularly large
role in the Zoroastrian scriptures in the Middle-Persian
language.[33] But the use of names already in Achaemenid
and Parthian times shows that the stem *baog-*, "save",
occupies a central place in the religious world of
ideas of the Iranian people. In favor of the high
antiquity of these conceptions, supported admittedly
in late Iranian texts, there is the circumstance that
they are encountered in the Upanishads. So, e.g.,

14

Śvetāśvatara Upaniṣad (1.1) opens with the question,

> What is the cause? Brahma?
>
> Whence are we born?
>
> Whereby do we live?
>
> And on what are we established?

And, as has already been indicated, the concept
of salvation, *mukti* or *mokṣa*, plays a central role in
the Upanishads.

The Principal Gnostic Motifs

1. Against this background we can now examine the
leading ideas in Gnosticism, and we begin with the
citation defining what *gnosis* entails. "What we were,
what we became" -- that question is answered in Gnosticism as follows: Man originally is a pure spirit,
but he became an earthly creature, shackled in matter.
"Where we were, whither we have been cast" -- this
question receives a similar answer: Man as a pure
incorporeal spirit dwelt in the heavenly regions with
God, but was plunged down into the world of matter,
darkness, and suffering. The mystery of salvation is
revealed in the answer to the two last questions,
"Whither we hasten, whence we are delivered". The
answer to this is clear: The spirit hastens back to
its heavenly dwelling with God, and is thus saved from
the world of matter and from the body, which is a part

15

of this world. Hence we can understand "what birth is, what rebirth". Birth means to be born here to this world which is in the power of matter. Rebirth is to be born anew as a free spirit to the divine world of light and imperishability.

The gnostic's picture of the true self and of the world thus coincides with the ancient macrocosm-microcosm speculation mentioned previously.[34] Man is only an image of the world. He himself consists of a higher element, the spirit, and a lower, the body. Similarly the universe consists partly of a spiritual element, viz. the sum of all spiritual beings, and partly of matter. The spirit's salvation from the prison of the body is a process in miniature, a detail of the larger process by which all spiritual elements in the world are saved from matter. The spirit, having gone forth from God, returns to him again. At this point we are confronted with the ancient principle concerning the relationship between the sum and its parts.[35]

In Manichaeism this principle is manifest in the fact that the Great Vohu Manah, *vahman* (or *manvahmēd*) *vazurg*, which includes in itself all *manah*-s, *vahmanan* according to the Manichaean terminology, appears as a savior-figure over against the individual *manah*-s. Here we have a motif that is altogether typical for Iranian religion and for Gnosticism, the idea of a savior who brings salvation to the spirits sunken in

16

matter and who thereby saves himself. To be sure, there are not lacking suggestions in the Upanishad texts to the effect that salvation is effected by "the Lord", *Īśvara* (e.g. *Śvetāśvatara Upaniṣad* 6.16).[36] But the motif does not occupy a central place in Upanishadic speculation. It is quite otherwise with the *avatāra* speculation to which we shall return later, but there the idea of the identity between the savior and the saved has largely disappeared.[37] In Iran, on the other hand, the salvation dogma itself consists precisely of the assertion that the Savior is identical to the sum of the saved. This is the positive side of the relationship. The negative side is seen in the fact that the Savior himself is in need of salvation. As the sum of all the spirits held captive in the bonds of matter, the Savior himself must be saved.[38] According to the gnostic view this itself is a fact of salvation, however various the different systems may be in details. Of course, we do have to take into account a considerable amount of variation between the different systems.

The merit of having brought some order into the bewildering multiplicity of gnostic views belongs to H. Jonas. With Jonas we make a systematic distinction between two types of gnosticism, the Iranian type and the Syro-Egyptian type. The former includes Manichaeism and Mandaeism, of which Manichaeism is especially typical of an Iranian religion,[39] as well as the view

17

represented in the "Hymn of the Pearl". The Syro-
Egyptian type includes all of the different forms of
Christian Gnosticism, as well as Hermetic Gnosticism.
The various forms of Islamic Gnosticism provide nothing
new, from the point of view of the phenomenology of
religion; these are only to be regarded as offshoots
of the two main types. In some cases, therefore, we
find the Iranian type represented, in other cases the
Syro-Egyptian. Common to both types is the pronounced
dualism between spirit and matter, between God and the
world, between the spheres of light and darkness, between life and death, and between good and evil. These
antitheses we know already from Indo-Iranian religion.[40]
But that which is typical and new in Gnosticism is the
consistent contention that matter is evil in and of
itself, in contrast to the spiritual, which as such is
divine. Even if we do find in Indian and Iranian forms
of religion certain impulses tending toward such a
consistent line of thought, nevertheless the lines of
differentiation are never drawn with such sharpness
as, finally, in Gnosticism.

2.   There is in the Syro-Egyptian type of Gnosticism,
however, an attempt to break through this consistent
dualism. *Viz.* it is speculated that from the highest
sphere of the divine, from God himself, there proceeds
a series of emanations, as rays from a light source.

These emanations, "aeons", which are "eternities" in the spatial as well as the temporal sense, represent the divine world, but in a descending scale the farther they are from the source of light. In various ways attempts are made to clarify, with the help of this aeon-speculation, how matter, evil, could come into existence through emanation from the spiritual, the good. We recall in this connection the ancient pantheistic speculation to the effect that the world is a product of a series of births from the body of the deity. This speculation lives on in Gnosticism, and is exploited for the purpose of constructing a tenuous bridge over the poles of the gnostic dualism. Thus the origin of evil is explained in such a way that it is ascribed to a fall within the divine sphere itself. Driven by a perverse inclination, the world-creating aeon, the Demiurge, brings forth the world. On the basis of this aberration, the world is perceived as a mixture of good and evil, of spirit and matter. And we recognize immediately in this idea of mixture the Iranian doctrine of *gumēčišn*. The main motivation of this doctrine of creation is, of course, to absolve the Deity of any kind of error, *viz.* that he intentionally created the world which is something evil. On the other hand, the attempt is made to preserve a connection between the creator of the world and the highest Deity. The gnostic does not regard the world-

ruler as a *completely* evil being.[41] Still, the question
as to *how* the perverse inclination of the Demiurge
could have arisen is not answered.

We have observed that this mixture of spirit and
matter, of good and evil, pertains just as much to the
macrocosm, the world, as to the microcosm, man. However
when the latter is in view, the gnostic speaks not of
two elements, spirit and body, but of three. Between
the spirit, *pneuma*, which is a purely spiritual element,
and the body, *soma* or *sarx*, which is purely material, he
interposes the soul, *psychē*, which is both spiritual and
material. In accordance with this tripartition within
man the whole race of mankind is divided also into three
classes, classified according to their relationship to
the spiritual. One thus speaks of the "spiritual" ones,
the *pneumatikoi*, the "psychic" ones, the *psychikoi*, and
the "bodily" ones, the *somatikoi* or *sarkikoi*.[42] Nevertheless it should also be noted that a hard and fast
gnostic terminology does not develop. With St. Paul,
for example, one finds all three terms, *pneumatikoi,*
psychikoi, and *sarkikoi* (e.g. 1 Cor. 2.14-3.1), but a
sharp trichotomy, in a gnostic sense, is not found in
his writings. Rather, Paul appears to use the terms
"psychic" and "sarkic" in the same sense, which according
to the gnostic schema would be erroneous. For the
gnostic the soul is, indeed, only a body or garment for
the higher spiritual ego.[43]

20

3. However, the terminology is most in flux when it pertains to the higher ego; indeed a strict terminology did not develop. In ancient Iran we can refer, among others, to the concept of *manah* and of *vyāna*.[44] In Manichaeism there remains the term *manah*, in the combination Vohu Manah, both when it applies to the cosmic term, the Savior-figure *Vahman* (or *Manvahmēd*) *vazurg*, and when it applies to the individual *manah*-s (pl. *vahmanān*).[45] But *vyāna*, under the form *gyān*, is the name for the soul as the lower life-principle in Manichaeism. The contrast between both of these principles appears clearly in a passage where the Great Manvahmēd, as individual Savior-figure, speaks to the man who is to be saved:

> And with me did he speak . . .
> and my "ego" was elevated
> and he talks to me:
> Well, soul, do not be afraid!
> I am your Manvahmēd,
> and a security and a seal,
> and you are my body,
> a garment [which I have put on]
> in order to frighten the forces.
> And I am your Light,
> the original effulgence, the Great Manvahmēd
> and a perfect security.[46]

The Great Manvahmēd is also a *manvahmēd* in man.
Indeed, the Savior says, "I am your manvahmēd." The
soul, *gyān*, is simply its garment, its body. Here we
find again the concordance in meaning between the two
symbols, "garment" and "body".[47] This interchange of
symbols is regularly recurrent in gnostic technical
terminology, of which we find traces in St. Paul. Paul
can speak on the one hand of a heavenly, pneumatic
body, which the Christian after death will put on at
the resurrection (1 Cor. 15.36-58). On the other hand,
in a context dealing with the resurrection, he says
that we groan with longing to be able to "put on over"
us (ἐπενδύσασθαι) the heavenly "building" prepared by
God in order that we be not found naked (2 Cor. 5:1-5).
Here a third term occurs, viz. "building"; otherwise
it is clearly the metaphor of the "garment" which
dominates the metaphorical language.[48]

4. We can see that according to Indo-Iranian conceptions the spirit at its heavenly journey receives the
garment, which in Iran, typically enough, can be called
the "Vohu-Manah garment" (*hān-i vohumanik vastrag*,
Dātastān i dēnīk 39.19) or *vohuman vastrag* (*ibid.* 48.9).[49]
The garment thus symbolizes the part of the higher ego
which remains in heaven. Only when the spirit puts on
this heavenly garment is salvation complete. We have
already referred to the famous "Hymn of the Pearl" in

22

the *Acts of Thomas*. One of the most beautiful motifs
to be found in that document is the meeting and reunifi-
cation of the king's son with his garment of splendor.
An especially interesting detail calls for comment:

> And the image of the king of kings
>
> was completely depicted all over it.
>
> --"Hymn of the Pearl" 86[50]

We have already seen that the Brahma garment,
which the soul receives according to Indian views, is
the world-mantle, and therefore the same as the body
of the Deity, the world, in which the Deity wraps himself as in a mantle. It is therefore quite natural
that the garment of splendor is here said to be deco-
rated with the picture of the King of Kings, *scil.* the
Deity himself. Seen from this perspective, therefore,
it is the world-mantle which the ascending soul puts
on after it has united with the Deity. We recall that
this is the part which returns again to the whole whence
it had gone forth. Apuleius, after he has undertaken
his heavenly journey during his initiation into the
mysteries, appears clothed in a garment, *Olympiaca
stola*, which is nothing else but that garment which is
also called the "Mantle of Heaven".[51] Reitzenstein
has correctly pointed out that the garment is also
conceived as an image. The king's son sees himself
reflected as in a mirror, clothed in the garment of splendor:

23

> Suddenly as I faced it,
>
> The robe was like a mirror of myself,
>
> I saw it all in my whole self
>
> And I faced my whole self in it,
>
> So that we were two in distinction
>
> And yet again one in one likeness.
>
> --"Hymn of the Pearl", 76-78

Instead of a meeting with the garment, one can find described how the soul goes to meet its image. The heavenly "body" can thus be regarded as a double, or twin-ego. In the Mandaean hymns for the dead, which constitute the cultic texts for the soul's "ascent", *massiqta*, the same formula recurs over and over again:

> I go to meet my image,
>
> And my image goes to meet me.
>
> It caresses and embraces me,
>
> As though I have returned again from captivity.
>
> --*Ginzā* L, 31 [52]

The captivity from which the soul returns is the prison of matter. This deliverance from captivity is constantly lauded in the gnostic texts.

The meeting between the redeemed ego and its heavenly counterpart is also given the symbolic form of a meeting with a young, beautiful maiden. This metaphor is encountered already in ancient Iran, in the famous 22nd *Yasht*, also called *Hadōxt Nask*:

24

At the close of the third night, at
daybreak, the soul of the pious man seems
to be among plants and sweet-smelling
things. There appears to him a wind
blowing from the south, from the southern
regions, a fragrant wind, more fragrant
than others. Catching the scent of
this wind the soul of the pious man
says, 'Whence blows this wind, the most
fragrant wind I have ever smelled?'
His own *daēnā* appears to him, coming
with this wind, in the form of a
beautiful maiden, beaming, white-armed,
robust, well-grown, stately, with fulsome
breasts, with upright posture, noble,
of illustrious lineage, with a fifteen-
year-old's appearance, with a body
as beautiful as the most beautiful
beings.

--Yasht 22.7-9[53]

The soul of the pious man asks who this beautiful
maiden might be, and receives the reply that she is
his own *daēnā*. The meaning of this word is somewhat
uncertain, but apparently, according to a new etymology,
is to be related to the Indian word, *dhéna*, which means
"cow", a designation also for "woman". Originally
dhéna has the meaning, "the nourishing", and can

25

therefore be used of the Indo-Iranian fertility- and mother-goddess, with whom the king celebrates the sacred marriage.[54] The soul's encounter with its *daēnā* is thus a heavenly counterpart of the *hieros gamos* ("sacred marriage"), and the gnostics often speak of the soul's embrace of its angel in the heavenly bridal chamber (cf. Irenaeus *Haer.* 1.21.3).

It is singular that Mohammed in the Koran uses a similar mode of speech when he speaks of how the souls after death "are paired together", *zuwwiǧat*, *scil.* "with the bodies" (Sura 81.7). Here, with reference to the mode of language predominant in Gnosticism and in the Syrian church, one might be able to think of *zuwwiǧat* in the literal sense, "to be married". Reitzenstein, on material grounds and precisely with reference to *Yasht* 22, had already conjectured for *daēnā* a meaning of "self", "I", in about the same sense as Greek *nous*, "mind".[55] Thus we can say that *daēnā*, like *manah*, is a designation for the higher principle of life, which, in contrast to the soul, we can call "spirit".

5. The *daēnā* now explains to the pious man's soul that through his good works he had made her all the more beautiful:

> I was lovely, and you made me more lovely,
> I was beautiful, and you made me more

beautiful,

I was desirable, and you made me more
desirable,

I sat upon a high place, and you made
me sit upon a higher,

Through this good thought, through this
good work, through this good deed.

--*Yasht* 22.14

We see from this passage that the higher ego in
heaven is dependent upon how its counterpart here below in the world carries out its good deeds. A perfect
parallel to this is found in the following passage
from the "Hymn of the Pearl", where the garment speaks:

I belong to the girdled among servants

For whom they reared me before my father,

And I also perceived in myself

That my stature grew according to his works.

--"Hymn of the Pearl", 91-92[56]

In the *Bundahišn*, therefore, it can be said:

O righteous man! I am the *daēnā* of
your work which you performed. When
you performed good deeds, I became this
way because of you.

--*Bundahišn* 37.6[57]

27

Thus there is a decisive correspondence between the part of man's higher self here below and that part which remains to dwell in the heavenly regions. The heavenly twin-ego includes in itself the treasure of good works which is gathered by the earthly ego here below. The heavenly beings which, in the "Hymn of the Pearl", bring the magnificent garment to the King's son, are therefore called "treasurers" ("Hymn of the Pearl" 79). Similarly, even the heavenly twin-ego, as the owner of this treasure, can be called "treasurer" (*Dātastān i dēnīk* 24.5). These terms play a large role in the gnostic literature, where "treasure", "treasure chamber", and "treasurer" constantly occur. Moreover in Mandaeism, as in Manichaeism, "treasurer" is a designation for the priest.[58] Even in Christian circles this conception of the heavenly treasure plays a large role, although as an immediate legacy from Judaism, wherein these gnostic-Iranian concepts had gained a footing (Matt. 6.19-21; 19.21).

6. Up to this point we have devoted our attention primarily to the individual soul which ascends to be reunited above with its heavenly self. But it is just as important to look at the other direction of motion, *viz.* the Savior's descent for the purpose of saving all the fragments which make up his collective self.

This descent of the Savior is an act of salvation which is performed both as a cosmological and a soteriological act. But it is also a process which is constantly repeated every time a soul responds to the Savior's call, and turns with him again to his heavenly origin.

When the mixture occurred -- the mixture of good and evil, spiritual and material, light and darkness -- and when the sense-perceptible world, based on this mixture, came into being, there then descended from the Deity a spiritual principle emanating from him, which we can designate his active aspect. We have already met this Savior-type in the person of the Great Vohu Manah. Vohu Manah represents the spiritual side of the Deity, corresponding to the Indian Ātman. But just as we could also find in India such a designation as Puruṣa, Man, used interchangeably with Ātman or Brahman, we find in Iran and in Gnosticism various terms which mean precisely "Man" as *terminus technicus* for the Savior-figure. What is emphasized thereby is that all men exist as parts of the Deity, who in turn is referred to as the "Great Man", a term which is encountered in Greek-speaking Gnosticism, μέγας ἄνθρωπος. In Manichaeism the designation "Primal Man" is used, in Syriac *nāšā qaḏmāyā* , in Middle-Persian *Gēhmurd*.[60] The latter term corresponds (as a result of the living development of the language) to the term *Gayōmart* in

29

the Zoroastrian texts. *Gayōmart* indeed preserves
the Avestan form *Gayō marta*.[61] Nyberg's studies have
demonstrated the plausibility of the identification of
the Savior-figure with the mythical Primal Man, as far
as the older Iranian religion is concerned. Very early
in the Zoroastrian community Zarathustra himself was
worshipped as the Primal Man.[62] However, Zarathustra
has also been venerated as a Savior-figure with yet
another term which, in contrast to the Primal Man
speculation stressing his connection with mankind,
underscores his connection with the divine sphere.
Zarathustra receives in the Zoroastrian Pahlavi scriptures the epithet, "Sent Out", *frēstak* (*Dātastān i
dēnīk* 37.43).[63] The term *frēstak* goes all the way
back to the time of the Gathas where we find *fraešta*
(*Yasna* 49.8).[64] To be sure Zarathustra is not alone
in receiving this term in the Avesta. An analogous
designation, *ašta*, which also means "Sent Out", is
given one of his reincarnations, *Astvatarta*.[65] At the
same time we note that in one passage in the Pahlavi
literature, in which Vohu Manah comes to Zarathustra
in order to allow him to lay aside the bodily garment
and make his way to Ahura Mazdā, Vohu Manah is called,
aštak (*Dēnkart* 7.2.60-61).[66] Furthermore, the *Dēnkart*,
in the so-called Zarathustra legend, speaks of Zarathustra's "coming into the world to be sent out for
Ohrmizd, and to be ruler and lord in the world"

30

(*Dēnkart* 7.2.49).[67] Since the *Dēnkart* in this case
renders Avestan terms, the conclusion is that Zarathustra was designated already in ancient Iran both as
Primal Man and as God's "Sent One".

In Manichaeism and Mandaeism, as in other gnostic
systems, the idea of the Savior as both Primal Man and
Apostle is taken up as a central theme.[68] Mani is the
"Apostle of Light", *frēstag-rošn*, the Savior-figure
sent out into the world by the Deity.[69] Mani functions
in this way as a kind of cyclic revelation of the
eternal Savior who constantly descends anew into the
world of matter in order to gather the spiritual elements
and restore them. Mani himself belongs to a series of
three such types: the Primal Man, the Living Spirit,
and the Third Messenger. All three are still only
variations of one and the same theme. And Mani himself
is an incarnation of the Great Nous, also called "Light-
Nous".[70] The Great Nous sits upon the ninth throne
in the heavenly world, while his earthly representative, the Apostle, called the "Apostle of Light" in
the Coptic texts, sits upon the ninth throne in the
earthly world.[71] We find the term *apostolos* used in
the Coptic Manichaean texts where the Iranian texts
have *frēstak*. The linking term is the Aramaic word
šelīḥā, "sent one"; it is this term that is used
originally of the "apostles" of the Christian gospel
in Aramaic-speaking circles.[72] Mani, the Apostle of

31

Light, has thus received the ancient Iranian designation for the Savior-figure. Just as in the *Dēnkart*
Vohu Manah could be called "Sent One" as well as Zarathustra, so also in Manichaeism Nous or Vohu Manah is
the "Sent One", just as Mani himself. Mani becomes
the "messenger", a term which is used interchangeably
with "apostle", when his heavenly twin-ego descends
and unites with him during the revelation that he brings
to him from the Deity. A being from the Light-world
comes to Mani, and this being is called "the twin",
and is thus nothing other than Mani's own twin-ego.[73]
Mani reported that he had received wonderful revela-
tions "from his twin, i.e. the Holy Spirit" (Euodius,
De fide 24). This twin-ego is thus identical with the
Spirit, according to the Christian terminology borrowed
in the western forms of Manichaeism, while in the
original Iranian-colored Manichaeism we find the Great
Vohu Manah. This meeting between the earthly apostle
and his heavenly twin-ego, which takes place in a
vision, has its Iranian prototype in the meeting between Zarathustra and Vohu Manah, portrayed in the
seventh book of the *Dēnkart*.[74]

7. The revelation brought through the agency of a
heavenly being, which is really the earthly apostle's
higher self, whereby the apostle becomes one with his
heavenly self -- this becomes a standard motif in many

32

gnostic systems. T. Andrae has compared such descriptions to the call of Mohammed by the angel Gabriel.[75] And it is surely a striking fact that the proclamation of Mohammed as "sent one", *rasūl*, is tied to the description of this meeting in the Koran.[76] By this meeting Mohammed becomes Allah's apostle. According to the tradition the angel says to Mohammed, "O Mohammed, you are Allah's Apostle and I am Gabriel!"[77] It is when the heavenly apostle descends to the earthly bringer of revelation that the latter becomes an "apostle" or "messenger" in the real sense of the words. These terms accordingly designate the gnostic Savior figure as one who is "sent out" from the heavenly world of light. Depending on whether one looks at his earthly or his heavenly manifestation, this figure can be designated in two ways. Mani's position is ambiguous. Sometimes he seems to want to serve merely as a human messenger who has been granted a revelation from the heavenly "Messenger". Sometimes he refers to himself as the Paraclete promised by Christ, the Holy Spirit.[78] This apparent contradiction occurs again to a certain extent with Mohammed. On the one hand it is well known that Mohammed constantly refused to be regarded as anything more than a man.[79] On the other hand, he gives himself the term, *rasūl Allāh*, "Apostle of God", which is the special designation for the Savior-figure, alludes to himself as the bearer of "Allāh's light"

33

(Sura 9.32-33; 61.8-9; 64.8), and speaks of "Allāh
and his apostle" almost as a unity.[80]

8.   The "Apostle" concept in early Christianity preserves much of this meaning. The Gospel of John is
dominated by the idea that Jesus is the heavenly "Sent
One".[81] Constantly the theme recurs, that Jesus has
been sent out in order to accomplish salvation. Nevertheless Jesus receives the epithet "Apostle" only in
one place in the New Testament, *viz*. in the Epistle
to the Hebrews. Yet one of the most common conceptions
in the gospels is that Jesus has been "sent out"
(cf. Luke 4.18 with Is. 61.1).[82] It is, of course,
also the case that the term "sent one" is a royal title
in the ancient Near East.[83] This royal term presents
within Semitic religion a point of contact with the
Iranian-gnostic concept of the sent-out Savior. Ploij
has maintained, quite correctly, that in the oldest
Christian tradition the term *apostolos* belongs to the
regular titulature pertaining to Jesus. However the
term soon falls out of use with reference to Jesus, and
comes to be limited to the Christian preachers of the
gospel.[84]

In the letters of Paul we can see in his constant
reference to his authority as apostle -- based on a
vision of the risen Savior -- a possible reminiscence
of the significant position that the "Sent One" really

34

holds.[85] Wensinck has also pointed out that in the
literature of the ancient church, "apostle" has a
meaning which transcends the one usually associated
with the word.[86] However it is in Syrian Christianity
that we find the concept "apostle" as a designation
for the divine Savior-figure, both in the Great Church
and in gnostic circles.[87]

9. Just as the terminology for the Savior-figure is
carefully fixed, his activity of salvation is also
portrayed in certain regularly recurring terminology.[88]
The souls held captive in matter are described as
having been plunged into a deep slumber, often specifically characterized as the heavy sleep of drunkenness.
In the "Hymn of the Pearl" it is related how the son
of the king sinks into a deep sleep, with the result
that he forgets his commission and his home.

> And I forgot the pearl
>
> For which my parents had sent me.
>
> And because of their heavy food
>
> I fell into a deep sleep.
>
> --"Hymn of the Pearl" 34-35

The King's son is awakened from this sleep by a
letter sent to him by his parents. The letter is
simply another symbol for the call of awakening which
the Savior, at his descent, sends out to the slumbering

35

soul.[89]   And in the "Hymn of the Pearl" the letter
is also transformed into a call of exhortation:

> It flew in the likeness of an eagle,
>
> The king of all birds,
>
> It flew and alighted beside me
>
> And became all speech.
>
> At its voice and the sound of its rustling
>
> I awoke and arose from my sleep.
>
> --"Hymn of the Pearl" 51-53

In a Manichaean text, the famous Zarathustra
fragment, it is stated,

> The Savior, the righteous Zarathustra,
>
> speaking with his own 'self':
>
> 'Heavy is the drunkenness in which you
>
> are sleeping,
>
> Wake up and look at me!
>
> Hail! from the world of peace,
>
> whence I have been sent out for your sake!'
>
> --*Mitteliranische Manichaica* III,
>
> p. 27, lines 86-95

This passage is of great phenomenological significance, for it shows the same relationship which
we were able to establish earlier: Zarathustra, founder
of the Zoroastrian community, is designated as the
Savior.[90]   That this motif of the slumbering soul has

great symbol-forming power was apparent to Reitzenstein,[91] who referred to a passage in the Epistle to
the Ephesians in this connection:

> Awake, O sleeper,
>
> And arise from the dead,
>
> And Christ shall give you light.
>
> --Ephesians 5.14 (RSV)[92]

As usual, Islam is an heir to earlier Christian-
gnostic conceptions. In the great encyclopedia com-
piled by the "Pure Brethren" in Bosra, one finds the
following regularly-recurring summons:[93]

> So wake up, O brother, from the sleep
>
> of negligence and the slumber of ignorance!

This motif appears often in Islamic gnosticism.
We can adduce another passage from the writings of the
"Pure Brethren":

> The resurrection of spirits means an
>
> awakening from the sleep of negligence and
>
> a waking from the slumber of ignorance, a
>
> life in the spirit of gnosis, and an
>
> emergence from the darkness of the world
>
> of natural bodies, a deliverance from the
>
> sea of matter and the captivity of nature,
>
> and an ascent to the levels of the world

37

of spirits, and a return to their spiritual
world, their place of light, and their
dwelling of life.

--*Rasā'il Ikhwān al-Safā'* III, p. 301[94]

10. The return to the original home takes place on
account of the Savior, who leads the soul, all souls,
with himself up to the world of light. Thus it is
described in the "Hymn of the Pearl" (75-97) how the
garment escorts the king's son on his journey home,
where he is welcomed joyfully. This welcome of the
returning one is portrayed often in the Manichaean
hymns. In one hymn, indeed, it is put in such a way
that we can get a glimpse into how the Iranian prototype to the "Hymn of the Pearl" must have described
the reception into the divine dwelling:

> The mother embraced and kissed him,
> 'You have returned, O exiled son,
> Hurry off, present yourself to the Light,
> for your relatives are longing for you
> exceedingly!'

--*Mitteliranische Manichaica* III,
p. 32, lines 92-98

In order for the return to be made possible, it
is necessary that the awakened Savior (the soul) be
furnished with fare for the journey, and accompanied

38

by a guide. Here we have contact with two additional
symbols which play a significant role in gnostic
technical terminology. "Fare" and "guide" have come
to be such usual metaphors both in Christendom and in
Islam that one is inclined to forget their original
technical meaning.[95]

The sojourn in the world of matter is referred
to as an "exile" also in Islamic gnosticism. "In its
condition as a stranger in this world" the soul re-
sembles a certain man who dwells in a foreign land
and there is seduced by a dissolute woman, "so that
he forgets his soul and his own well-being and his
own land from which he withdrew and his relatives,
together with whom he had grown up."[96]

In Christian-gnostic, Manichaean, and Mandaean
literature, the metaphor of the ship, skipper, and
cargo is often used to depict the soul's return to
the heavenly world.[97] In the following text from the
writings of the "Pure Brethren", this motif also
occurs, taking the form of a detailed allegory:

> And know, O brother, that the body is
> like the ship, the soul like the captain,
> and the good deeds like the cargo and the
> possessions of the merchant, and the world
> like the sea, and the days of life like
> the journey, and death like the landing,

and the other world like the merchant's
city, and paradise is the profit and God
-- exalted be he -- is the king who
requites.[98]

In summary, one can find again in the writings
of the "Pure Brethren" all of the familiar phrases
of the gnostic technical language.

Still others are encountered in Islamic eschatology,
which borrowed so many features from Iran, e.g. the
metaphor of the beautiful maiden that meets the righteous
soul after death -- even though the maiden has changed
her sex and become male![99] In somewhat modified form
this description is encountered also in the writings
of the "Pure Brethren".[100]

11. As we have seen earlier, in India one finds
speculation concerning a god's *avatāra*-s, or "descents".[101]
This speculation is tied especially to the figure of
the god Vishnu. Vishnu comes down to earth in a
"descent" every time the truth requires aid in order
to triumph. The *Bhagavad Gītā* explains that Vishnu
in this way is born again:

Many are My past lives and thine, O Arjuna;
I know all of them but thou knowest them
not, O oppressor of the foe. Although
unborn, although My self is imperishable,

40

            although I am Lord of all beings, yet

            establishing Myself in My own (material)

            nature, I come into being by My own

            mysterious power (*māyā*). Whenever there

            is a decay of righteousness and a rising

            up of unrighteousness, O Bhārata, I send

            forth Myself. For the preservation of

            good, for the destruction of evil, for

            the establishment of righteousness, I

            come into being in age after age.

            --*Bhagavad Gītā*, 4th song[102]

   In the case of Vishnu one reckons with a number
of various avatars, usually 10, among which the most
important are his descents as the gods Rāma and Krishna.
When the current world-cycle is concluded, Vishnu is
born again as Kalki and frees the world from evil.[103]

   In certain types of Buddhism -- and certainly not
exclusively within the northern canon -- one encounters
a plurality of Buddha, somewhat reminiscent of the
avatāra speculation. The number of Buddhas varies
from 7, which is most common, to 27 and 81.[104] There
is also, in Buddhism, the well-known Boddhisattva
speculation, in which the numbers have a tendency to
be astronomical. The sūtra, *Saddharmapuṇḍarīka*, "Lotus
of the True Doctrine", thus presents a group of 80,000
bodhisattvas, of which, nevertheless, only 25 are

                              41

discreetly counted by name.[105] Yet, though these
bodhisattvas and Buddhas are worshipped as deities in
the folk religion, they are not really designated as
incarnations of a single deity as are the avatars of
Vishnu. Ideas of rebirth do appear in the Buddhist
speculation, nevertheless. Buddha manifests himself
anew at every time "when men have become unbelieving,
unwise, ignorant, careless, fond of sensual pleasures."[106]
Here we have, as Thomas points out, an exact counterpart to the aforementioned idea of Vishnu's rebirth
when truth and right suffer distress.[107] In this way
one arrives at the conclusion that it is one and the
same Buddha who reveals himself in various reincarnations
in different periods of time. Great is the joy among
the gods, when after a seemingly interminable interval,
a Buddha again manifests himself. The gods break forth
in jubilation:

> Marvelous it is, O lord, how after such
> a long time you have today manifested
> yourself in the world. During fully
> eight thousand aeons had this world
> of the living been without Buddha.
>   --*Saddharmapuṇḍarīkasūtra* 7.32[108]

12. In the gnostic systems of the Near East we often
find ideas of a cyclical revelation of the Savior-

figure. According to Mani's teaching, the eternal Savior descends at various times into the world of matter, in order to accomplish his work of salvation. The technical term for this figure, as we have found, is "Apostle" or "Messenger". Mani identifies himself with this saving being, which is his own higher self. Mani also reckoned with other earthly incarnations of the heavenly Savior. The Arabic scholar Al-Biruni cites from one of Mani's books this illuminating pronouncement:[109]

> Wisdom and deeds have always from time
> to time been brought to mankind by the
> apostles of God. So in one age they
> have been brought by the apostle called
> Buddha to India, in another by Zara-
> thustra to Iran, in another by Jesus
> to the West. Thereupon this revelation
> has come down, this prophecy in this
> last age through me, Mani, the apostle
> of the God of truth to Babylonia.

As T. Andrae has said, "the summons has come to various peoples in various times. The great religions in the west, India, and Persia contain one and the same divine truth; their founders are all God's envoys."[110] We can add: These sent-ones are also all incarnations of one and the same heavenly being.

43

Andrae shows how similar views must have been known to Mohammed, and that his consciousness of call is a continuation of the doctrine of the apostle of divine revelation to different peoples at various times.[111] Within Islam the doctrine of the cyclical revelation also came to play a large role in Shi'ah. In Shi'ah, however, it was restricted most immediately to apply to the Imam, though at first the revelation was allowed to have a more universal character. The Sect of the Seven, or Ismā'īlīyah, for example, reckon with a series of incarnations of the divine principle, the world-intellect, $'aql$, which manifests itself in Adam, Noah, Abraham, Moses, Jesus, Mohammed, Ismā'īl, and the latter's son Muhammad ibn Ismā'īl.[112] The Iranian heresiarch al-Muqanna', who appeared after the death of Abū Muslim, follower of the Abbasids, and who belonged to his faithful, set forth far-reaching claims. According to the best-preserved source, he declared,

> I am your God and the God of the whole
> world. I call myself by whatever name
> I wish. I am he who manifested himself
> in the creation in the guise of Adam,
> and later in the guise of Noah, later
> in the guise of Abraham, later in the
> guise of Moses, later in the guise of

Jesus, later in the guise of Muhammed,

and later in the guise of Abū Muslim,

and finally in the appearance you now

behold.[113]

This line is maintained later in Shi'ah and all of its various branches. The Shi'ite Imam preserves the outline of the gnostic Savior-figure,[114] and takes his place in the series of incarnations in which the heavenly "Apostle" reveals himself from time to time. The gnostic conception of the Savior, which at decisive points strongly influenced Christianity, still lives on with a vigorous life within the Shi'ite sect's belief in the Imam.

13. But Gnosticism continues its life also within Christendom. Various sects such as the Bogomils[115] and the Cathari[116] preserved and spread the gnostic views. The spiritual movements of the middle ages salvaged an abundance of gnostic material. This was carried further by the various baptist sects of the 16th century, by spiritual mystics, by the Behmenists and other related movements. Among the 18th-century Freemasons, Rosicrucians, Swedenborgians, and St. Martinists, many of the ancient gnostic ideas are still preserved.

In Sweden we have a genuine gnostic in the romantic poet Eric Johan Stagnelius. In his poetry

all of the gnostic technical terminology lives on with
the full force of the gnostic experience itself.

A few citations from his poetry can illustrate
the phenomenological resemblance. First of all, the
clearly dualistic picture of the world:

> So is there above the heavens
>
> Encompassed by the golden-rayed sun
>
> Where the flaming stars sparkle in the
> Azure
>
> Another more luminous world?
>
> So is there also one of darkness and
> delusion
>
> Vying with the other in conflict?
>
> > --"Wladimir den store" [Vladimir the Great]

The two worlds, that of light and that of darkness, are thus seen to be situated in conflict with
each other. The perceptible, material world exists
as a mixture between these two spheres which balance
one another here in the universe.

> An eternal balance between light and
> darkness
>
> A tree of knowledge of good and of
> evil is the world.
>
> > --"Martyrerna" [The Martyrs]

The divine sphere is put in stark contrast to

the perceptible world, when Perpetua[117] breaks forth
full of longing:

> O limpid light, not shadowed by mixture!
>   --"Martyrerna"

The word "mixture" is of interest here, for it
is a technical term in the gnostic language.[118]
Stagnelius returns to this concept of "mixture" when
he says,

> In this world, foul and fair
> I see in eternal mixture battling.
>   --"Till Tron" [To Faith]

The soul has plunged, or been lured, from the
sphere of light into the dark and foggy world of matter.
The poet portrays this situation in a typical passage
as follows:

> Beautiful as the beam in your blue eyes,
> Shone the soul of yore in the Cherub choir,
> Beside the lofty throne of God,
> Glowing sweetly as the flower of your cheeks,
> Radiant as your lips, until the godly soul
> Sank, seduced from her heaven down
> To the dust where peril dwells.
>   --"Kärleken" [Love]

Here it should be pointed out that the words

47

"dust" and "peril" are technical terms with Stagnelius,
who always uses them as epithets of the material world.

The soul's sojourn in the material world is described, in the usual gnostic manner, as wandering,
drunkenness, slumber, and captivity.

The soul's separation from God is a wandering:

> Sighing she wandered,
>
> Among murky phantoms
>
> In the Zodiac's night.
>
> --"Dialog"

Of Psyche the poet says:

> Bewitched by matter's dark delusion,
>
> With flowing locks and teary cheeks,
>
> Psyche pining follows Amor's tracks.[119]
>
> --"Kärleken"

It is not only Psyche, but also the individual
soul that wanders about in the material world.

> Straying in deserts, shackled in irons . . .
>
> Shut up by Time in his prison,
>
> Does not the lonely spirit have a heaven?
>
> --"Himmelen" [Heaven]

The soul's wandering is often described by the
poet as a wilderness wandering:

Straying in deserts, shackled in irons . . .
Psyche in exile trudges through the
barren deserts of the world.

> --*Samlade Skrifter* [Collected Works] XCIII

In the works of Stagnelius, one also encounters
"drunkenness" and "slumber" as symbols for the soul's
sojourn in the material world. The soul drinks a
potion of oblivion:

But not a single soul from Splendor's
kingdom
Descended to the misty Pluto-halls of
Time,
But did not drink oblivion from the
gloomy Lethe
Whose billows break between the poppy
fields.
And so I drank. Thus sank unseen distances
In the blood-red west my childhood heavens,
And in the hemisphere that now arose
The World-ruler's stars, threatening
and enraged,
Flashed forth with diamond sceptres.
All was forgotten -- yet raged in the soul
A mystic pang, much like the dreams of
sickness.

> --*Samlade Skrifter* XCII

The departure from the higher world can, with
reference to this potion, be portrayed under the metaphor of intoxication. When the soul is offered to
leave the "World-ruler's" legacy in order to return
to its heavenly home, the answer is:

> Hold on to your pearls -- know that the
> Zodiac's god
> Sells not so easily his beloved bride,
> Intoxicated with earthly wines,
> She was sold for gold and rubies.
>
> --"Tårarne och blodet" [Tears and Blood]

This potion the poet calls "the mead of peril".
The soul is asked if it has forgotten its homeland:

> Have you forgotten the gentle majesty
> Revealed by homeland's climes?
>
> --"Varningen" [The Warning]

The soul itself bewails the forgetfulness in which
it has been seized:

> Ah! So long a guest in dust's deep valleys
> I have forgotten the Reality that is,
> My sisters and brothers in heaven's halls,
> And the very punishment that keeps me
> captive here.
>
> --"Rodnaden" [Blushing]

Forgetfulness and drunkenness has such strong
power over the soul that its existence can be described with the metaphor of deep sleep:

> With wet cheeks slept the soul,
>
> Consumed by age-old sorrow,
>
> In the Demiurge's gloomy court,
>
> In a star-watched fortress.
>
> --"Vårsånger" [Spring Songs]

Captivity is the most common of all symbols for
the union of the soul with the material element. Thus
the Demiurge boasts:

> From Eden's bed of roses,
>
> And from her bridegroom's arms,
>
> Shackled in the sense-world
>
> I shut poor Psyche up.
>
> Never shall she slip away.
>
> Time's serpent I have bidden to guard
>
> Her heavenly figure in the cosmic night.
>
> --*Samlade Skrifter* XLVII

Anima, the soul, can longingly sigh:

> Only released from my prison would I be.
>
> The tears! The blood!

The heavenly envoy descends to awaken the slumbering soul, as depicted in the following passage

51

which follows the lines from "Vårsånger" cited above:

> Come, said a whispering Zephyr,
> Wake up, O beautiful bride!
> Here, arriving in his flower-chariot
> Is the young god of Spring.

This passage should be compared to the question that Anima raises when she sorrowfully remembers her heavenly origin and her kin above in the world of light. She calls out, asking,

> How lives the blessed
> Immortal host
> Above in the ether?
> Ah! Heavy is my head
> From the vapors of earth.
>
> --"Dialog"

In still other poems of Stagnelius one finds a whole raft of gnostic conceptions, e.g. descriptions of the process of salvation itself. But it would lead us too far afield to illustrate these motifs also.[120]

The Gnostic Conception of Time

In Greek thought Time is understood as a cyclical process.[121] This view of time stands in marked con-

52

trast to the Christian conception of time.[122] In the
latter, time can be compared to a straight line along
which all of human history plays itself out. In this
understanding, time does not only have a beginning and
an end; it also has, through Christ's coming into the
world, an absolute center.[123]

In gnostic reflection, we are confronted with an
altogether unique conception of time. This has been
demonstrated in a well-documented study by H.-C.
Puech.[124] He shows that the relationship between the
temporal and the non-temporal is seen very differently
by the gnostic, as compared to the Greek view. Since
for the gnostic the cosmos itself is something evil,
so also is time, which is connected with the cosmos.
Time, as created by the Demiurge, is "at best a cari-
cature of eternity."[125] Thus Gnosticism renounces
time as it renounces the world.

As for the relationship between the Christian
concept of time and the gnostic concept, this can be
seen in what happens within Christian Gnosticism.
Christian Gnosticism radically lifts Christianity out
of time. To be sure, Jesus has entered the cosmos as
Savior, and thereby has entered into the category of
time. But he stands isolated. He has no historical
connection with the Jewish people, for example.
According to the gnostic view, Jesus is not a human
being endowed with a human body. No, the gnostic

Savior breaks into the cosmos and into time from above. He can, in fact, be called "Jesus Christ" or something else; it matters not.[126]

Thus Gnosticism, in its conception of time, is independent of either Greek or Jewish ideas.[127] The gnostic revelation "shatters history into bits".[128]

FOOTNOTES

* Chapter 16 (pp. 279-306), "Den gnostiska inställningen", in *Religionens värld*, 3rd ed. (Stockholm, 1971), hereinafter cited *Phenomenology* (Sw.) = Chapter 17 (pp. 480-516), "Die gnostische Einstellung", in *Religionsphänomenologie* (Berlin, 1969), hereinafter cited *Phenomenology* (Ger.).

1. On pantheism, see *Phenomenology* 48 ff. (Sw.), 93 ff. (Ger.).

2. On the origin of Gnosticism, see the important collection of papers from the Messina Congress, *Le origini dello gnosticismo*, ed. U. Bianchi (Leiden, 1967), hereinafter cited *Le origini*. For the position taken in this essay, see also G. Widengren, "Der iranische Hintergrund der Gnosis", *ZRGG* 4 (1952) 97-114.

3. The following discussion is based on H. Oldenberg, *Die Lehre der Upanishaden und die Anfänge des Buddhismus* (Göttingen, 1923) 76 ff.

4. *Ibid.*, 77 ff.

5. *Ibid.*, 100.

6. *Ibid.*, 100 f.

7. Quotations from the Upanishads are taken from the English translation by R. Hume, *The Thirteen Principal Upanishads,* 2nd ed. (London, 1931).

8. Oldenberg, *op. cit.*, 101-105.

9. See e.g. *ERE* X, art. "Rāmānuja".

10. S. Wikander, *Vayu* (Lund, 1941), p. 47.

11. *Ibid.*

12. See W. Bousset, "Die Himmelsreise der Seele," *ARW*
    4 (1901) 136-169, 229-273 (r.p. Darmstadt, 1960),
    especially comprehensive in its treatment of the
    Indo-Iranian and Manichaean, as well as the Man-
    daean material.

13. G. Widengren, *The Great Vohu Manah* (Uppsala, 1945),
    84 ff.

14. For the *Sānkhya* system see S. Konow, *Hinduismen* I
    (Stockholm, 1927), p. 44, and J. Gonda, *Die
    Religionen Indiens* I (Stuttgart, 1963), 302 ff.
    On the question of salvation in the older Indian
    religion see H. Güntert, *Der arische Weltkönig
    und Heiland* (Halle, 1923), 242 ff., and S. Rohde,
    Deliver Us From Evil (Lund, 1946).

15. See *ERE* VIII, art. "Mokṣa".

16. Cf. *ERE* XI, art. "Salvation", esp. pp. 134 f.

17. Wikander, *op. cit.*, 26 ff.

18. *Ibid.*, 42 ff.

19. Cf. *Phenomenology*, 264 ff. (Sw.), 456 ff. (Ger.).

20. That position was vigorously maintained by R.
    Reitzenstein, and is even better established now.
    It is the fundamental error of certain recent works
    that these basic insights have not been properly

taken into account, e.g. C. Colpe, *Die religions-geschichtliche Schule* (Göttingen, 1961). Cf. G. Widengren, "Die religionsgeschichtliche Schule und der iranische Erlösungsglaube", *OLZ* 58 (1963), 544-546.

21. It is assumed here that there was a Mazdā faith already, before Zarathustra. Cf. G. Widengren, *Die Religionen Irans* (Stuttgart, 1965), 14 f., 147 f.

22. H. Nyberg, "Questions de cosmogonie et de cosmologie mazdéennes," *JA* 219 (1931), 76 ff.; G. Widengren, *Die Religionen Irans*, 284 f.; *Phenomenology* 267 (Sw.), 460 (Ger.). See also Widengren, "The Principle of Evil in the Eastern Religions", *Evil*, trans. R. Manheim and Hildegard Nagel (Evanston, Ill., 1967), 38 f.

23. Nyberg, *JA* 214 (1929), p. 206; *Bundahišn* ch. 1 (German tr. in Widengren, *Iranische Geisteswelt*, Baden-Baden 1960, 58-71).

24. Nyberg, *JA* 219 (1931), p. 77. The struggle between Ahura Mazdā and Ahra Mainyu is a characteristic theme in Zoroastrianism since the time of the Gathas; see Nyberg, *Die Religionen des alten Iran* (Leipzig, 1938), 102 ff.

25. On the contrast between life and non-life see Nyberg, *Die Religionen des alten Iran*, p. 103, where *Yasna* 30.4 is quoted (cf. also the tr. in

Widengren, *Iranische Geisteswelt*, p. 150): "As
these two spirits came together, they created
the first Life and Non-Life." On this Nyberg
says (*ibid*.): "Life or Non-Life are therefore
the great antitheses of man's world." On the
opposition of Light and Darkness, one can refer
to *Yasna* 31.20, where it is stated that whoever
is a follower of truth, *aša*, is far away from
the grief of sorrow and darkness. Cf. Nyberg,
ibid. 179 f. In the darkness dwell the evil
powers, *daēvas*, *Yasna* 57.18. Darkness and death
are equated with evil, from which Mithra's
dwelling-place is free, *Yašt* 10.50. On darkness
as the place of the evil powers, see also
Vīdēvdāt 5.62; 18.76; 3.35; 19.30; and *Yašt* 6.4.
See now also Widengren, *Evil*, 34 f.

26. Nyberg, *ibid*., 20.

27. If we assume, with Nöldeke, that it goes back to
a Pahlavi version; see Th. Nöldeke, *Burzoes Ein-
leitung zu dem Buche Kalila wa Dimna* (Strassburg,
1914), p. 24; cf. G. Widengren, *Iranische
Geisteswelt*, 94-107.

28. Cf. R. Zaehner, "A Zervanite Apocalypse" (pt. 2),
BSO(A)S 10 (1939-42), 621 f.; E. Benveniste, "Le
Témoignage de Théodore bar Kônay sur le zoro-
astrisme," *MO* 26 (1932), 185 ff.; G. Widengren,
"Les origines du gnosticisme," in *Le origini*, 44

ff.; and "Primordial Man and Prostitute: A
Zervanite Motif in the Sassanid Avesta," in
Studies in Mysticism and Religion (Festschrift
G. Scholem), ed. R. Werblowsky (Jerusalem, 1967),
337-352.

29. A Valentinian formula, from *Excerpta ex Theodoto*
ch. 78. The same formula is found in the Valentinian *Evangelium Veritatis, CG* I ("Jung Codex")
22.13-18: "Thus he who possesses *gnosis* knows
whence he has come and whither he is going; he
knows as one who has been drunk but is awakened
from his drunkenness." On the formula, see H.
Jonas, *Gnosis und spätantiker Geist* I, 2nd ed.
(Göttingen, 1964), p. 261, and *The Gnostic
Religion,* 2nd ed. (Boston, 1963), p. 45. The
pioneering work of Jonas is fundamental for the
following discussion.

30. Quotations from this catechism are taken from A.
Freiman, "Pandnāmak i Zaratušt" (Text and German
tr.), *WZKM* 20 (1906), pp. 238, 241 f., 269. Such
catechism-type questions occur in other places
in the Pahlavi literature. The antiquity of this
literary type is clear from *Yasna* 43.7-8. From
a history-of-religions perspective a useful com-
parison can be made with the question formulae
among the Islamic *futuwwah* societies; see H.
Thorning, *Beiträge zur Kenntnis des islamischen*

59

Vereinswesens (Berlin, 1913), p. 65. See further
E. Norden, *Agnostos Theos* (Leipzig, 1929, r.p.
Darmstadt, 1956), 99 ff.; J. Kroll, *Die Lehren
des Hermes Trismegistos* (Münster, 1914), 372 ff.;
A. Delatte, *Études sur la littérature Pythagori-
cienne* (Paris, 1915), 274 ff.

31. We are confronted here with symbols from ancient
    Iranian culture and religion. The heavenly world
    is described as a city. This is also the case
    in certain Buddhist texts; cf. the expression
    "Nirvana-City", *nŭrvanŭ kantha*, E. Leumann,
    Maitreyasamiti (Strassburg, 1919), p. 64, 100.

32. See e.g. *Mēnōk i Xrat* 2.2, 67, 196; 57.9.

33. See, in addition to the citations above, *Mēnōk i
    Xrat* 43.15. On salvation in Iranian religion
    see Widengren's forthcoming essay in the Brandon
    Memorial Volume (in press).

34. See above, p. 4. On the macrocosm-microcosm
    speculation see *Phenomenology*, 55 f. (Sw.), 103
    f. (Ger.).

35. Cf. *Phenomenology*, 54 f. (Sw.), 102 f. (Ger.).

36. See further *ERE* VIII, art. "Mokṣa", where other
    examples are given.

37. See below, pp. 40 ff.

38. The fundamental analysis of this aspect of
    Gnosticism was provided by R. Reitzenstein in his
    Die Göttin Psyche (Heidelberg, 1917).

39. Cf. *Phenomenology*, 52 ff. (Sw.), 98 ff. (Ger.), and esp. G. Widengren, *Mani and Manichaeism* (London, 1965), 43-73, where most of the Iranian elements in Mani's doctrine are discussed.

40. See above, p. 10 f.

41. Cf. *Phenomenology*, p. 267 (Sw.), p. 460 (Ger.). On the Syro-Egyptian form of Gnosticism as a weakening of the consistent dualism of the Iranian form, see G. Widengren, "Les origines du gnosticisme," in *Le origini*, 40-42. On the Demiurge cf. H. Jonas, "Delimitation of the Gnostic Phenomenon -- Typological and Historical," in *Le origini*, 101, 103 f.

42. Cf. R. Reitzenstein, *Die hellenistischen Mysterienreligionen* (Leipzig, 1927, r.p. Darmstadt, 1966), 326 ff.

43. Jonas, *Gnosis und spätantiker Geist* I, 186 f., 208 f.; Reitzenstein, *Mysterienreligionen*, 355 ff., 411 ff.

44. Cf. *Phenomenology*, 55-57 (Sw.), 103-106 (Ger.). In the Pahlavi text, *Handarz i Āturpāt i Mahraspandān*, ch. 123 (numbering acc. to Harlez, *Muséon* 6, 1887, p. 75), it is stated: "The *mind* is the preserver and protector of the *soul*, and the mind is the savior and helper of the *body*." This saying is important for middle-Iranian anthropology, for we see clearly here a trichotomy

of mind, soul, and body.

45. Cf. *Phenomenology*, 57 (Sw.), 106 (Ger.).

46. G. Widengren's English translation of a Parthian
    Manichaean hymn fragment from Turkestan (T II D
    178 III) in *The Great Vohu Manah and the Apostle
    of God* (Uppsala, 1945) 17 f. (Parthian text also
    given). Cf. also E. Waldschmidt and W. Lentz,
    Die Stellung Jesu im Manichäismus (Berlin, 1926),
    p. 113, and especially M. Boyce, *The Manichaean
    Hymncycles in Parthian* (London, 1954), p. 140
    (Parthian text) - 141 (Engl. tr.).

47. Cf. *Phenomenology*, 248 f. (Sw.), 434 (Ger.);
    also R. Reitzenstein, *Mysterienreligionen*, 179.

48. On these passages see, on the one hand, H.
    Lietzmann, *An die Korinther I, II* (Tübingen, 1923),
    84 ff. and 117 ff., and on the other hand Reitzen-
    stein, *Mysterienreligionen*, 335 ff., 350 ff.,
    355 ff. On the metaphor of the "building" cf. P.
    Vielhauer, *Oikodome* (Karlsruhe, 1940), 106 ff.
    On the Iranian side see H.W. Bailey, *Zoroastrian
    Problems* (Oxford, 1943), p. 209, and the text from
    Zātspram, ch. 29. The same interchange of the
    two symbols, "garment" and "dwelling" (or
    "building") recurs often in the *Rasā'il Ikhwān
    al-Safā'*; cf. G. Widengren, "The Gnostic Technical
    Language in the Rasā'il Ihwān al-Safā', *Proceedings
    of the IVth Congress of Arabic and Islamic*

Studies (Madrid, 1972), p. 183 with n. 1.

49. See above, p. 8 , and Widengren, *The Great Vohu Manah*, 50 ff.

50. Quotations from the "Hymn of the Pearl" are based largely on the English translation by A. A. Bevan, *The Hymn of the Soul Contained in the Syriac Acts of St. Thomas* (Texts and Studies V:3, Cambridge, 1897, r.p. Nendeln, 1967), with Syriac text. Cf. the German translation by G. Widengren in *Iranische Geisteswelt*.

51. Apuleius, *Metamorphoses*, 11.24. Cf. Reitzenstein, *Mysterienreligionen*, 42 f., 350 f.; cf. also G. Widengren, "Heavenly Enthronement and Baptism. Studies in Mandaean Baptism", *Religions in Antiquity. Essays in Memory of Erwin Ramsdall Goodenough*, ed. J. Neusner (Leiden, 1968), p. 570.

52. From Lidzbarski's German translation, *Ginzā* (Göttingen, 1925), p. 559, lines 29-32. On this passage cf. Reitzenstein, *Mysterienreligionen*, p. 178.

53. From the Swedish, following the text division of SBE, vol. 23, p. 315 f. For the comparable German version, cf. G. Widengren, *Iranische Geisteswelt*, 171-175; also his remarks in *OLZ* 58 (1963), 539-543.

54. Cf. *Phenomenology*, 143 (Sw.), p. 252 (Ger.). The "new" etymology was suggested by S. Hartman,

of Lund University. For Syriac conceptions see Narses' Homilies on the Soul, A. Allgeier, "Ein syrischer Memrâ über die Seele in religions-geschichtlichen Rahmen", *ARW* 21 (1922), 360 ff., where the relationship between soul and body are described as in terms of the relations between man and wife. Fundamental for the history-of-religions perspective are the works of R. Reitzen-stein, *Die Göttin Psyche*, and *Das Märchen von Amor und Psyche bei Apuleius* (Leipzig, 1912).

55. Reitzenstein, *Mysterienreligionen*, p. 410.

56. For the translation "girdled", i.e. "armed", see Widengren, "Der iranische Hintergrund der Gnosis," p. 109; cf. also Widengren, "Le symbolisme de la ceinture," *Iranica antiqua* 8 (Melanges R. Ghirshman, Leiden, 1968), 133-155. In Mandaean literature corresponding expressions are *zriza* and *mzarza*; see M. Lidzbarski, *Mandäische Liturgien* (Berlin, 1920), 225:1-2, and *Ginzā* (Göttingen, 1925), p. 295, where it is said that the Great (Life) girdled Anosh-Uthra and sent him out to awaken the slumbering from their sleep. The word "servant", in the Syriac text ʿaḇdā, indicates the vassal and can therefore be used about a prince. On the Mandaean passages see Widengren, "Le symbolisme," 150 f.

57. Pahlavi text and English tr. (here adapted), J.

64

Modi, "An Untranslated Chapter of the Bundahesh",
JRASB 21 (1900-03), p. 61.

58. On Mandaeism see the indices in Lidzbarski,
Ginzā, under *Schatz, Schatzhaus, Schatzmeister*.
On Manichaeism see F. Andreas, *Mitteliranische
Manichaica aus Chinesisch-Turkestan* II (Berlin,
1933), ed. W. Henning, p. 33 (324) n.3. See
further Widengren, *The Great Vohu Manah*, Additional
Note No. 1, pp. 84 ff.

59. Reitzenstein's works have been of pioneering
quality also here. A summary of the earlier
discussion is given by C.H. Kraeling, *Anthropos
and Son of Man* (New York, 1927).

60. R. Reitzenstein and H. Schaeder, *Studien zum
antiken Synkretismus aus Iran und Griechenland*
(Leipzig, 1926), p. 209, n.5; Andreas, *Mitteliranische Manichaica* I (Berlin, 1932), p. 48.

61. H. Nyberg, *Hilfsbuch des Pehlevi*, Glossar
(Uppsala, 1931), p. 80; *Die Religionen des alten
Iran*, p. 481, n. to p. 391.

62. Nyberg, *Religionen*, 30, 302 f., 392; somewhat
more cautiously Widengren, *Die Religionen Irans*,
99 f.

63. Cf. Widengren, *The Great Vohu Manah*, 64 ff.

64. See C. Bartholomae, *Altiranisches Wörterbuch*
(Strassburg, 1904), 975. Cf. Widengren, *The
Great Vohu Manah*, 66.

65. See Bartholomae, *op. cit.*, 215, *astvat.ereta-*. Cf. Widengren, *The Great Vohu Manah*, 62.

66. On this text see C. Salemann, *Manichaeische Studien* (Petersburg, 1908), 130 f., and H. Reichelt, *ZII* 2 (1923), 237 f. Cf. Widengren, *The Great Vohu Manah*, 60 ff.

67. This passage is a resumé of a lost Avestan version.

68. On Mandaeism, cf. Reitzenstein-Schaeder, *op. cit.*, 326 ff., and see the index in Lidzbarski, *Ginzā* under *Bote, Gesandter*. Cf. further R. Reitzenstein, *Das iranische Erlösungsmysterium* (Bonn, 1921), 48, 52, 54.

69. On the term *frēstag-rošn*, see e.g. Andreas-Henning, *Mitteliranische Manichaica* II, Glossar p. 66 (357), under *frēstag*. Cf. Widengren, *The Great Vohu Manah*, 29 f.

70. See *Kephalaia* I:1, ed. A. Böhlig (Stuttgart, 1940), p. 35, lines 21-22: The Light-Nous is "Father of all the Apostles". The Envoy, *presbeutēs*, has come forth from his Nous, p. 76, line 20. Cf. Widengren, *The Great Vohu Manah*, 20 ff.

71. See *Kephalaia* I:1, p. 82, lines 22-24. Cf. Widengren, *ibid.* p. 22.

72. This term *š^elīhā* also occurs in the Mandaean literature, where the term *šlīhā* is applied to the Savior figure. See e.g. Lidzbarski, *Ginzā*,

66

p. 15, lines 21 ff.; 89, lines 6 ff. Cf. G.
Widengren, *Muhammad. The Apostle of God and His
Ascension* (Uppsala, 1955), 55 ff.; *The Ascension
of the Apostle and the Heavenly Book* (Uppsala,
1950), ch. 4.

73. See in addition to the Euodius passage G. Flügel,
Mani (Leipzig, 1862), p. 84, 140; Widengren, *The
Great Vohu Manah*, 25 ff., and *Mani and Manichaeism,*
26-28. The twin ego of Mani also occurs in the
newly discovered Greek Mani Codex from Cologne;
see A. Henrichs and L. Koenen, "Ein griechischer
Mani-Codex," *ZPE* 5 (1970), esp. 161 ff.

74. See above, p. 30, and Widengren, *The Great Vohu
Manah*, 60 ff., 71. Cf. the correspondence in
the *Acts of Thomas* between Jesus and Thomas, and
the interesting story of the descent of the Holy
Spirit to Jesus in *Pistis Sophia*, ch. 61.

75. T. Andrae, *Muhammad* (Stockholm, 1930), 127 ff.;
cf. Andrae-Widengren, *Muhammad* (Stockholm, 1967),
pp. 111 ff. It is typical in the description
that the heavenly being appears in gigantic form.
This motif has its original locus in the description in the *Dēnkart* (7.3.51), where it is stated:
"And it seemed to him that Vahuman was as tall
as a spear of three men's length." Also for
Mohammed, Gabriel appeared so tall that he stood
astride the horizon. Cf. Andrae-Widengren,

Muhammad, 68; Widengren, *Muhammad, the Apostle of God,* 125 f.

76. In the Koran we have the following noteworthy passages: Sura 44.12-13; 81.19-23; 26.143, 178, 193. Especially important is the last passage, Sura 26.192-195: "Truly it is the revelation of the Lord of all Being, brought down by the Faithful Spirit upon thy heart, that thou mayest be one of the warners, in a clear, Arabic tongue." (Arberry's English tr., London, 1955). Cf. with *al-rūḥ al-ʾamīn,* "faithful spirit", v. 178: *rasūlun ʾamīnun,* "faithful messenger". Cf. further Andrae-Widengren, *Muhammad,* 134 f., and Widengren, *Muhammad, the Apostle of God,* 8 ff.

77. See Ibn Hišam, *Das Leben Muhammeds,* tr. G. Weill (Stuttgart, 1864), p. 114; English tr. A. Guillaume, *The Life of Muhammad* (Oxford, 1955), p. 106. On the passage cf. Widengren, *Muhammad, the Apostle of God,* p. 124 ff.

78. See Andrae-Widengren, *op. cit.,* 115.

79. See especially T. Andrae, *Die Person Muhammeds im Glauben seiner Gemeinde* (Stockholm, 1918), 8 ff.

80. See especially Widengren, *Muhammad, the Apostle of God,* 11 f., 34, 170.

81. R. Bultmann, "Die Bedeutung der neuerschlossen mandäischen und manichäischen Quellen für das

Verständnis des Johannesevangeliums," *ZNW* **24** (1925), 100-146.

82. Cf. D. Ploij, *Studies in the Testimony-Book, the Apostle and Faithful High Priest Jesus* (Amsterdam, 1933), p. 46.

83. *Phenomenology*, 205 ff. (Sw.), 363 ff. (Ger.); G. Widengren, *The Ascension of the Apostle and the Heavenly Book* (Uppsala, 1950), 19 f.

84. Ploij, *loc. cit.*

85. H. Windisch, "Die Christusepiphanie vor Damaskus (Act 9, 22 und 26) und ihre religionsgeschichtlichen Parallelen", *ZNW* 31 (1932), 1 ff., concentrating on a different motif, the conversion of a persecutor of the Deity by a vision through which he is struck blind and rendered powerless; cf. 2 Macc. 3, the Heliodorus episode. On the "apostleship" of Paul, see also Windisch, *Paulus und Christus* (Leipzig, 1934), esp. pp. 143 ff.

86. A.J. Wensinck, "Muhammed und die Propheten," *Acta Orientalia* 2 (1924), 171 ff.

87. Cf. *Acts of Thomas*, chs. 9, 20, 31, 42, 44, 49, etc., and G. Phillips, *The Doctrine of Addai* (London, 1876), p. 6, where the "apostle" Addai is called "sent one". Cf. further Widengren, *Muhammad, the Apostle of God*, 65 ff.

88. See H. Jonas, *Gnosis und spätantiker Geist* I, 113 ff., and *The Gnostic Religion*, 68 ff. On the "Hymn

of the Pearl" and its Iranian, specifically Parthian, background, see Widengren, "Der iranische Hintergrund der Gnosis".

89. Jonas, *Gnosis und spätantiker Geist* I, 120 ff., and *The Gnostic Religion*, 74 f., 80 ff., 119 f.

90. Cf. above, p.

91. *Erlösungsmysterium*, p. 6, 135 ff.

92. K.G. Kuhn has compared Ps. Sol. 16.1-2 in this connection; see "Der Epheserbrief im Lichte der Qumrantexte", *NTS* 7 (1960-61), 334-346. This passage belongs to the same complex of ideas, but seems to represent a weakening of the ideas found in Ephesians. The conception of Christ as a manifestation of light, a *Sol Salutis*, in the dark realm of the dead is totally absent from the Psalms of Solomon, for we do not find there a mention of the Messiah in a role similar to that in Ephesians. See also the important articles by P. Pokorný, "Epheserbrief und gnostische Mysterien", *ZNW* 53 (1962), esp. 187 f., and G. MacRae, "Sleep and Awakening in Gnostic Texts", in *Le origini*, esp. 506 ff.

93. F. Dieterici, *Die Naturanschauung und Naturphilosophie*, 2nd ed. (Leipzig, 1876), p. 52.

94. *Rasā'il Ikhwān al-Safā'*, 4 vols. (Beirut, 1957); German tr. of this passage in F. Dieterici, *Die Lehre von der Weltseele* (Leipzig, 1872), p. 98.

Other passages from Islamic Gnosticism are found in H. Schaeder, "Die islamische Lehre vom voll-kommenen Menschen," *ZDMG* 79 (1925), p. 232.

95. On these symbols, see Widengren, *The Great Vohu Manah*, p. 79, 87 f.; and cf. above, p. f. On their use in the *Rasā'il Ikhwān al-Safā'* see Widengren, "The Gnostic Technical Language", cited above n. 48.

96. Text, *Rasā'il Ikhwān al-Safā'* III, p. 50, lines 14-23, translated (somewhat abbreviated) by F. Dieterici in *Die Anthropologie der Araber* (Leipzig, 1871), p. 132. On the motif of "alienness" in Gnosticism see Jonas, *Gnosis und spätantiker Geist* I, 96 f., and *The Gnostic Religion*, 49 ff. See further Widengren, "The Gnostic Technical Language".

97. Cf. G. Widengren, *Mesopotamian Elements in Manichaeism* (Uppsala, 1946),

98. *Rasā'il* III, p. 44, tr. Dieterici, *Anthropologie*, p. 127. Cf. the Manichaean allegory, W. Henning, "The Book of the Giants", *BSO(A)S* 11 (1943), p. 59.

99. M. Wolff, *Muhammedanische Eschatologie* (Leipzig, 1872), Arabic text p. 36, tr. p. 63 f. On the relationship between Iranian and Islamic eschatology cf. L.H. Gray, "Zoroastrian Elements in Muḥammedan Eschatology!", *Muséon* 21, N.S. 3 (1902) 153-184. See further Widengren, *Iran and*

Islam (Jordan Lectures 10, 1971, in press).

100. *Rasā'il* II, p. 42 f. (text). Dieterici, *Die Naturanschauung*, 52 f.; cf. Dieterici, *Anthropologie*, 107 f. = *Rasā'il* III, p. 36, lines 1 ff. The Paradise-Maiden in Islam belongs to this same context; she symbolizes the higher ego of the earthly soul. On this see E. Berthels, *Islamica* 1 (1924-25), 263-287. Cf. above, pp. 24 ff.

101. Above, p. 17; cf. *Phenomenology*, 271 (Sw.), 465 (Ger.).

102. English tr. by E. Deutsch, *The Bagavad Gītā* (New York, 1968), p. 54 f.

103. S. Konow, *Hinduismen* I, 54 ff. Cf. *Phenomenology*, 269 (Sw.), 463 (Ger.).

104. See E. Thomas, *The History of Buddhist Thought*, 2nd ed. (London, 1951), p. 142, 147, 186, 193. On the relationship between Gnosticism and Buddhism see E. Conze, "Buddhism and Gnosis", *Le origini*, 651-667.

105. Thomas, *op. cit.*, 180.

106. *Ibid.*, 184.

107. *Ibid.*, 185.

108. German tr. in M. Winternitz, *Der Mahāyāna-Buddhismus* (Tübingen, 1930), p. 18.

109. Cf. Andrae-Widengren, *Muhammad*, p. 114. The following passage is from the book dedicated to King Shāpur I, *Šāhpuhrakān*, as quoted by Al-

Biruni (ca. 1000 A.D.), *Athar ul Bākiya*, English
translation (here adapted) by C.E. Sachau, *The
Chronology of Ancient Nations* (London, 1879),
p. 190; for the Arabic text see Sachau, *Chronologie
alter Völker* (Leipzig, 1878), p. 207.

110. Andrae-Widengren, *Muhammad*, 150 f.

111. Cf. *ibid.*, 122 ff., and Widengren, *Muhammad, the
Apostle of God*, chs. 1-2.

112. I. Goldziher, *Vorlesungen über Islam* (Heidelberg,
1925), p. 243.

113. Mohammed Nerchakhy, *Description topographique et
historique de Boukhara*, ed. C. Schefer (Paris,
1892), p. 64. On Muqannaʿ see G. Sadighi, *Les
mouvements religieux Iraniens au IIe et au IIIe
siècle de l'hégire* (Paris, 1938), 163 ff., and
Widengren, *Die Religionen Irans*, 354.

114. Cf. *Phenomenology*, 335 f. (Sw.), 557 f. (Ger.).

115. H.-C. Puech and A. Vaillant, *Le traité contre les
Bogomiles de Cosmas le prêtre* (Paris, 1945).

116. H. Söderberg, *La religion des Cathares* (Uppsala,
1949).

117. Perpetua is a famous early Christian martyr whose
death is recorded in *Passio ss. Felicitatis et
Perpetuae*. See R. Knopf and G. Krüger, *Ausge-
wählte Märtyrerakten* (Tübingen, 1965), 35-44, for
Latin text and bibliography.

118. See above, pp. 10, 19.

119. For the myth of Psyche and Eros (Amor) see
Apuleius, *Metamorphoses*, 4.28-6.24. Cf. R. Reit-
zenstein, *Das Märchen von Amor und Psyche bei
Apuleius* (Leipzig, 1912).

120. On Stagnelius see especially Widengren, "Gnostikern
Stagnelius", *Samlaren*, New Series 25 (1944), 115-
178, where a detailed analysis is given. See
further S. Cederblad, *Studier i Stagnelii
romantik* (Uppsala, 1923), 187 ff.

121. Cf. *Phenomenology*, 272 (Sw.), 469 (Ger.).

122. Cf. O. Cullmann, *Christ and Time*, rev. ed.
(Philadelphia, 1964).

123. Cf. H.-C. Puech, "Temps, histoire et mythe dans
le christianisme des premiers siècles," *Pro-
ceedings of the Seventh Congress for the History
of Religions* (Amsterdam, 1951), p. 38, where he
lays special stress on this point.

124. "La gnose et la temps," *Eranos-Jahrbuch* 20 (1952),
57-113; English tr., "Gnosis and Time," *Man and
Time* (Papers from the Eranos Yearbooks 3, New
York, 1957), 38-84.

125. Puech, "Gnosis and Time," p. 61, in contrast to
the classical Greek view expressed by Plato,
Timaeus, 37c-38a.

126. On the relative insignificance of the name given
to the gnostic Savior, see Widengren, *Mani and
Manichaeism*, 158.

127. The same judgment applies to all of the chief
     motifs in Gnosticism. The "Hymn of the Pearl"
     and the Mandaean writings are completely free of
     Christian elements. It would carry us too far
     afield to enter into controversy with certain
     contributors to the Messina Congress volume, *Le
     origini*, but major agreement could here be ex-
     pressed with the positions taken in the articles
     of A. Adam, A. Böhlig, G. Gnoli, H. Jonas, and
     H. Schoeps, to name a few. Furthermore, it should
     be emphasized that the "Hymn of the Pearl" is not
     only not Christian, but is also pre-Christian; cf.
     Widengren, *OLZ* 58 (1963), 546 f. Of course, it
     should not be argued that Jewish and Christian
     elements are not assimilated into Gnosticism,
     especially Jewish. But then there are also
     Platonic, Orphic, Egyptian, and any number of
     other pagan themes, too, for which one can refer
     to the volume, *Le origini*, itself. See especially
     the interesting concluding essay by U. Bianchi,
     716-746, in which the various perspectives are
     analyzed closely.

128. Puech, "Gnosis and Time," p. 63.